Countries Around the World

Greece

Jilly Hunt

Heinemann Library
Chicago, Illinois

www.capstonepub.com
Visit our website to find out more information about Heinemann-Raintree books.

To order:
☎ Phone 888-454-2279
⌨ Visit www.capstonepub.com
to browse our catalog and order online.

Edited by Laura Knowles
Designed by Victoria Allen
Original illustrations © Capstone Global Library Ltd 2012
Illustrated by Oxford Designers and Illustrators
Picture research by Mica Brancic
Originated by Capstone Global Library Ltd
Printed and bound in China by CTPS

15 14 13 12 11
10 9 8 7 6 5 4 3 2 1

Library of Congress Cataloging-in-Publication Data
Hunt, Jilly.
  Greece / Jilly Hunt.
     p. cm.—(Countries around the world)
  Includes bibliographical references and index.
  ISBN 978-1-4329-6098-8 (hb)—ISBN 978-1-4329-6124-4 (pb) 1. Greece—Juvenile literature. I. Title.
  DF717.H78 2012
  949.5—dc22   2011015417

Acknowledgments

We would like to thank the following for permission to reproduce photographs: Alamy pp. **11** (© David Hancock), **14** (© Plastic Photo), **23** (© Steve Bentley), **25** (© Alisa Andrews), **32** (© ACE Stock Limited), **33** (© RIA Novosti), **35** (© Hemis/hemis.fr/Franck Guiziou); Corbis pp. **9** (© Hulton-Deutsch Collection), **21** (epa/© Simela Pantzarzi), **28** (Hemis/© René Mattes), **31** (© Gail Mooney); iStockphoto p. **17** (© Iraklis Klampanos); Photolibrary pp. **16** (Bios/Denis Bringard), **26** (Michael Good), **39** (Jon Arnold); Rex Features p. **30** (Everett Collection); Shutterstock pp. **5** (© Mikael Damkier), **7** (© Rechitan Sorin), **13** (© Maugli), **15** (© Mordeccy), **18** (© Benjamin Albiach Galan), **19** (© Guryanov Andrey Vladimirovich), **24** (© Panos Karapanagiotis), **29** (© Digivic), **46** (© Christophe Testi).

Cover photograph of cupolas with the caldera volcano in the distance in the Greek island of Santorini reproduced with permission of Shutterstock/© Petros Tsonis.

We would like to thank Daniel Block for his invaluable help in the preparation of this book.

Every effort has been made to contact copyright holders of material reproduced in this book. Any omissions will be rectified in subsequent printings if notice is given to the publisher.

Disclaimer
All the Internet addresses (URLs) given in this book were valid at the time of going to press. However, due to the dynamic nature of the Internet, some addresses may have changed, or sites may have changed or ceased to exist since publication. While the author and publisher regret any inconvenience this may cause readers, no responsibility for any such changes can be accepted by either the author or the publisher.

Contents

Some words are printed in bold, **like this**. You can find out what they mean by looking in the glossary.

Introducing Greece

What do you think of when you think of Greece? Sunny holidays? Greek food? Or maybe you think of ancient Greece with its classical temples? Greece has a fascinating past of ancient civilizations, wars, and invasions. It is a country rich in history and culture.

Today, Greece is a lively multicultural society. It has had recent **migration** from the Balkans, Africa, Asia, the United Kingdom, and Germany. Tourism is a very important part of the Greek economy with over 18 million tourists visiting every year. That's more than the total population of Greece!

About 11 million people live in Greece. That is quite a small population for its size, compared to other countries in Europe. More than half of the people in Greece live in the country's three largest cities. Athens is the capital of Greece and is by far the largest city. If you were to travel away from the big cities and out into the countryside you would find small villages perched on hillsides or the whitewashed houses of little fishing villages. Greece has some remote, rural communities that have hardly been touched by the technologies of the 21st century.

The Greek alphabet

The Greek language uses a different alphabet than we do, known as the Greek alphabet. This alphabet has developed over time from a number of different alphabets.

How to say...

hello	γεια σας	(yeea-sas)
my name is...	με λένε	(meh lene)

The islands of Santorini are the remaining parts of an erupted volcano. The islands' buildings are built up the steeply sloping land.

History: An Ancient Civilization

The modern state of Greece is only about 183 years old. However, Greece has an ancient past.

Between 500 and 400 BCE, the Greek culture was one of the most advanced in the ancient world. Athens was at the heart of this civilization and was where some of the best artists, writers, leaders, and thinkers in history lived. Some famous ancient Greek thinkers were Pythagoras, Socrates, and Plato. Pythagoras was a **philosopher** and mathematician who lived in the 6th century BCE. Socrates lived in the 5th century BCE and was a famous thinker. Plato was his pupil and wrote down his teacher's work.

The society of Athens was the world's first **democracy**. This meant that citizens could vote and help decide how the city should be run. Women, foreigners, and slaves, however, were not allowed to vote.

Daily life

Life in ancient Athens was very different depending on who you were. Only wealthy men could enjoy the cultural life, such as going to the theater. Women looked after the home and children. Boys would go to school from about seven years old, but girls would be expected to help around the house.

The ancient Greeks built elaborate temples for their gods and goddesses. The Parthenon was built as a temple to the goddess Athena, and part of it is still standing today.

In 337 BCE, Alexander the Great became ruler of Greece. He spread Greek culture over his vast **empire**, which included Egypt, Iran, and parts of Turkey and India. He died of fever in 323 BCE and his empire was divided up. Greece was eventually taken over by the Roman Empire. As the Roman Empire declined in the 400s CE, Greece became part of the **Byzantine Empire**. Greece was then taken over by the **Ottoman Empire** in the 1450s.

ALEXANDER THE GREAT (356–323 BCE)

Alexander III was known as Alexander the Great. He was king of Macedonia, which was an ancient kingdom near Greece. He died when he was just 33, but by then he had already **conquered** most of the world known to people at that time.

Greek War of Independence

The modern country of Greece as we know it today began with its independence from the Ottoman Empire in 1829, following a seven-year war. A Greek **monarchy** was created in 1832 with the backing of larger European powers. The monarchy was strengthened under the reign of King George I, who ruled for 50 years from 1863 to 1913.

Over the next century, Greece expanded to include all of present-day Greece and parts of present-day Turkey. After losing the Greco-Turkish War of 1919–1922, Greece had to give back part of its territory. After the war, people moved back to their own country's territory. About 1.3 million Greeks left Turkey and about 350,000 Turks left Greece. Suddenly there were a lot more people living in Greece.

This map shows the areas under Ottoman rule at the height of the empire in the late 1600s, and where modern-day Greece and Turkey lie within this region.

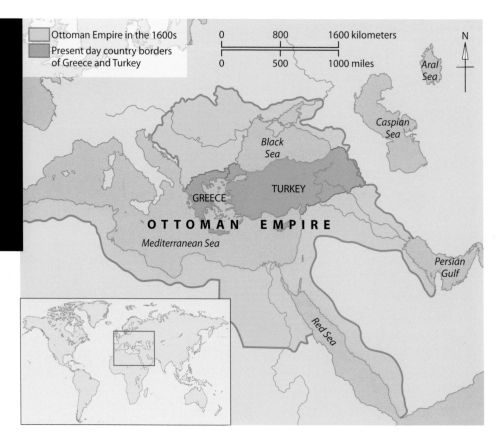

Ottoman Empire in the 1600s
Present day country borders of Greece and Turkey

0   800   1600 kilometers
0   500   1000 miles

N

Aral Sea

Caspian Sea

Black Sea

TURKEY

GREECE

OTTOMAN EMPIRE

Mediterranean Sea

Persian Gulf

Red Sea

Troubled times

After losing the Greco-Turkish War, there were many different rulers in Greece. There was also an **antiroyalist revolution**, which led King George II to abandon the throne in 1923. The leaders of the revolution took control and held an **election**. However, in 1926, the prime minister, Theodoras Pangalos, declared himself **dictator**. He was overthrown a year later, and former prime minister Eleuthérios Venizélos returned. He was defeated in 1932, and in 1935 King George II became king again. In 1936, General Ioannis Metaxas took control of the government and began a dictatorship with royal approval. He remained in power until his death in 1941.

Greece faced more trouble during World War II. It was invaded by Italy in 1940 and **occupied** by Germany in 1941–1944. More than 300,000 Greeks died during the occupation. About 80 percent of Greece's Jewish population died—about 60,000 people. When the Germans left the country, the Greek government returned. But in 1946 a **civil war** began. The **communists** had been fighting against the Germans and did not want to **disband** their forces. They wanted to rule Greece. The Greek civil war lasted until 1949.

KING GEORGE II

King George II was born on July 20, 1890, in Tatoi, near Athens. He became king in September 1922. He was **exiled** from Greece twice. The first time was on December 19, 1923, following a revolution. A change of government allowed him back in October 1935. King George II was exiled for a second time after the German invasion in 1941. A vote by the people of Greece allowed him to return in September 1946, and he ruled until his death on April 1, 1947.

Greece and Turkey

Greece and Turkey have always had a difficult relationship. There have been disputes over the control of the island of Cyprus. The British controlled Cyprus, but more than 75 percent of the population was Greek, and there was a large Turkish minority. Greece felt that Cyprus should be part of Greece, and Turkey wanted it to be part of Turkey. In 1960, an agreement was finally reached among Great Britain, Greece, and Turkey by which Cyprus would become an **independent republic**.

In 1974, the Greek dictator, Dimitrios Ioannidis, was involved in organizing an attempted **coup** against President Makarios of Cyprus because he wanted to control Cyprus. Turkey seized the opportunity to invade Cyprus and established an area of Turkish control in northern Cyprus. Ioannidis wanted Greece to go to war with Turkey. But Greek citizens and the leaders of other countries did not want this to happen. Ioannidis's regime was over. Today, Turkey still controls part of northern Cyprus, which it calls the Turkish Republic of Northern Cyprus. However, this name is not recognized by any other country in the world.

A return to democracy

Following the collapse of Ioannidis's regime in 1974, Greece had **democratic elections** and became a **parliamentary republic**. The monarchy was abolished. Former prime minister Konstantinos Karamanlis and his New Democracy Party won the election.

Greek people are very proud to be Greek. These people are celebrating Greece's win of the European Football (what we call soccer) Championship in 2004.

Greece joins the EU

In 1981, Greece joined what is now the **European Union (EU)** and became its 10th member. EU membership helped Greece in 2010 when its economy nearly collapsed. The EU, along with the **International Monetary Fund (IMF)**, have loaned Greece billions of euros to help rescue its economy. The Greek authorities have started trying to improve the situation by introducing **economic reforms**. However, there have been protests and strikes against some of these reforms.

YOUNG PEOPLE

A study in 2007 for the Council of Europe found that for most young people in Greece, belonging to the EU means freedom to travel, study, and work anywhere in the EU.

Regions and Resources: Mountains and Islands

Greece is in southeastern Europe. It is made up of mainland Greece and more than 2,000 islands. It has land borders to the north and northeast with Albania, the Former Yugoslav Republic of Macedonia, Bulgaria, and Turkey. Including its islands, Greece has a long coastline of more than 8,450 miles (13,600 kilometers). It is surrounded by the Ionian Sea, the Mediterranean Sea, and the Aegean Sea.

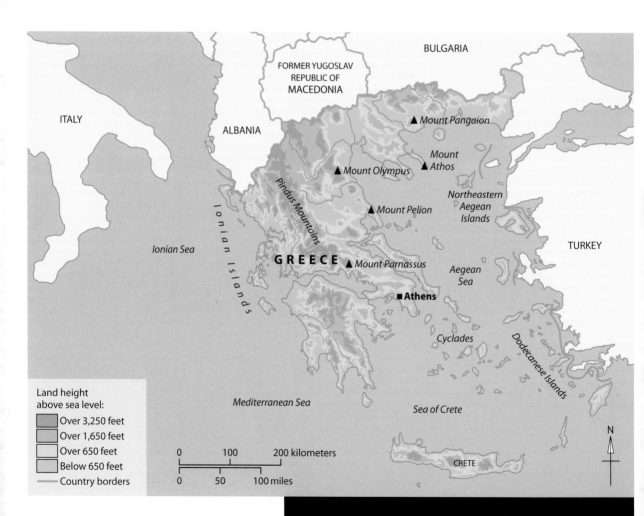

Land height above sea level:
- Over 3,250 feet
- Over 1,650 feet
- Over 650 feet
- Below 650 feet
- Country borders

0   100   200 kilometers

0   50   100 miles

N

Greece covers about 51,000 square miles (132,000 square kilometers) of land. This map shows the main geographical features of the country.

Mountains

Mountains make up about 80 percent of Greece. The highest peak is in the Mount Olympus range and is called Mytikas. It is 9,570 feet (2,917 meters) high. The ancient Greeks believed that this was the home of **Zeus**, the most powerful of the Greek gods.

The mountains of Greece are young and are still in the building stage. This means there are many earthquakes. There is also some volcanic activity.

Greek islands

The Greek islands are grouped by which sea they are in. There are the Aegean islands off the east coast in the Aegean Sea, and the Ionian islands off the west coast in the Ionian Sea. The island of Crete is south of the mainland in the Mediterranean Sea. It is the largest of the Greek islands and a popular place for vacationers.

This is the Greek island of Symi. There are over 2,000 islands in Greece. The islands make up about 20 percent of the land area of Greece.

Climate

The summers in Greece are usually hot and dry, and the winters are mild and rainy. In the mountain regions there is snow during the winter months. In the hot, dry summers, forest fires are a danger.

Daily life

The warm climate in Greece means that open-air cinemas are popular in the summer. Indeed many indoor cinemas close for the summer. The open-air cinemas have seats arranged around the screen and are often in a garden-like setting with a lot of flowers. At an open-air cinema you can get something to eat or drink while watching the film. It is traditional to eat dried sunflower or pumpkin seeds.

Natural resources

Greece's natural resources include **bauxite**, lead, zinc, nickel, magnesite, and marble.

One of Greece's most important resources is the country itself. Millions of tourists visit each year because of the weather, beautiful scenery, and history.

Agriculture and fishing

Only a small part of Greece can be farmed (about 30 percent), but it is still an important part of the Greek economy. In the warmer coastal areas and on the islands, crops such as olives and grapes are grown. In the north, crops such as wheat and corn are grown. Greece also produces wine, herbs, and nuts.

Sheep and goats are kept in the mountain regions. One popular Greek sheep and goats' cheese is known as Feta. With so many islands, it is not surprising that the fishing industry is also an important part of the economy.

Greece is famous for its olives. This olive grove is in northern Greece.

Industry

Greece produces food, drinks, chemicals, textiles, clothing, and transportation equipment. However, industry in Greece is not as strong as it is in some other European countries. The shipping industry is very important in Greece. The **merchant fleet** is one of the largest in the world. Greek ships are mainly **bulk carriers** that carry cargo between different countries. Greece's high-technology and telecommunications industries developed during the 1990s and are important in the modern world.

Wildlife: A Variety of Life

Greece is rich in wildlife. To help protect this wildlife, Greece has a number of national parks, including Olympus National Park, Pindos National Park, and Parnassos National Park. Greece also has two marine parks that protect areas of the sea and coast and the wildlife that lives there.

Most of the national parks are mountain ranges covered in forests and are home to a variety of birds. On the island of Crete is the Samaria Gorge National Park, which is home to the rare Cretan goat. The Prespes National Park covers two freshwater lakes that also go into Albania and the Republic of Macedonia.

Animal life

The mountain ranges and coastal areas are home to a variety of animals. The inland mountain ranges, **gorges**, and cliffs are homes to eagles and vultures. Bears, wolves, wild boars, **lynxes**, and deer live in the mountain forests. On the warmer, southern coasts live **jackals**, wild goats, and porcupines. The seas around Greece are home to numerous fish **species**, whales, dolphins, seals, and sea turtles.

Plant life

Greece has over 6,000 species of flowering plant. Some of them cannot be found anywhere else in the world. There are primroses, peonies, anemones, tulips, and violets.

If you were to visit Greece in spring, you might be lucky enough to see one of the wild orchid species in flower.

Dancing bears

Europe's largest population of brown bears lives in the forests of northern Greece. Until it was banned in 1969, some people would make money from "dancing bears." The bears were made to dance by burning their front feet on hot coals while their masters played the tambourine. The bears were so traumatized by this experience that they would dance whenever they heard the tune. The ARCTUROS Bear Sanctuary at Nimfeo, Florina, looks after bears that cannot be released back into the wild because of the injuries and distress they have experienced.

YIANNI BOUTARI

Yianni Boutari is a successful winemaker who helped set up a sanctuary for rescued bears that could not be released back into the wild. "There was a law which outlawed dancing bears but no system for taking the bears and nowhere for them to go," Boutari explained. In 1992, the ARCTUROS Foundation was formed to look after these bears and to conserve the brown bear and its habitat in Greece. The ARCTUROS bear sanctury has a team of 16 staff, 40 associates, and another 40 volunteers.

There are thought to be around 160 wild brown bears left in Greece today.

Endangered Loggerhead turtles

The Loggerhead turtle is an **endangered species**. One of the turtle's natural nesting places is the beaches in the bay of Laganas on the Greek island of Zakynthos. The adult females return at night to lay their eggs on the beach where they were born. They bury their eggs in the sand and, about two months later, the baby turtles hatch and scuttle to the sea for safety.

The Loggerhead turtles are affected by human behavior, such as noise and bright lights. Their nests can also be damaged by tourists using the beaches. In 1999, a National Marine Park (NMPZ) was established to help protect the Loggerhead turtles. It is the first marine park in Greece and covers 52 square miles (135 square kilometers). It has been difficult for the Greek authorities to protect an area that has a large local population as well as a lot of tourists each year. However, the staff and a team of volunteers patrol the turtle-nesting beaches night and day. They give out information to tourists about the turtles, count the turtle nests, and keep people away from nesting sites.

Young turtles instinctively head for the moonlight and the safety of the sea when they hatch out of their eggs. They can get confused if they see the bright lights of a resort.

Dadia Forest Wildlife Reserve

The Dadia Forest Wildlife Reserve is in northern Greece, near the city of Alexandroupolis. It is home to the black vulture. It is on one of the two main bird **migration** routes in Europe and is an important place for rare birds. In the 1980s, there were only 25 individual black vultures breeding in the Dadia forest. The black vulture was thought to be a threatened species. After a lot of **lobbying**, a section of the forest was made into a protected zone by the **WWF** and the World Conservation Union. In this zone, **logging** was banned, what tourists could do was limited, and projects such as new roads were stopped.

Setting up the wildlife reserve and the controlled use of the forest for the local people has meant that some people are not able to use the forest for activities they have done in the past. However, many are now involved with the ecotourist ventures, such as the escorted tourist walks through the forest.

The black vulture is one of the largest birds of prey in the world.

Infrastructure: What Makes Greece Work?

A country's infrastructure is the set of systems and services that are needed for everyday life to run properly. The infrastructure includes power and water supplies, transportation and communication systems, schools, and hospitals. The Greek government runs the country and makes sure everything works smoothly.

Government and politics

Greece is a **parliamentary republic** with a president and a prime minister. The Greek government is elected by popular vote. This happens every four years. The leader of the political party that wins the most votes becomes the prime minister. The prime minister has the most power. The president selects the people to run the different government departments.

This map shows the 13 administrative regions that make up Greece.

FORMER YUGOSLAV REPUBLIC OF MACEDONIA

BULGARIA

EASTERN MACEDONIA AND THRACE

CENTRAL MACEDONIA

ALBANIA

WESTERN MACEDONIA

Thessaloniki

THESSALY

EPIRUS

GREECE

NORTHERN AEGEAN

IONIAN ISLANDS

Ionian Sea

WESTERN GREECE ● Patra

CENTRAL GREECE

Aegean Sea

TURKEY

■ **Athens**

ATTICA

PELOPONNESUS

Mediterranean Sea

SOUTHERN AEGEAN

Sea of Crete

N

| 0 | 100 | 200 kilometers |
| 0 | 50 | 100 miles |

CRETE

Currency

Like many countries in Europe, Greece is in the **Economic Monetary Union (EMU)**. This means the Greek currency is the euro (€).

Economic conditions

In 2009–2010, Greece faced some serious financial difficulties. In May 2010, the **IMF** and **Eurozone governments** gave Greece emergency loans worth €110 billion (about $159 billion) so that it could repay its debts. The Greek government has announced tough spending cuts and an increase in taxes. This has not been popular with the general public, and there have been violent protests.

Extra financial pressure is being put on Greece by an increase in **migrants** crossing the border from Turkey. Many migrants are also coming from Afghanistan and Albania. Some want to travel through Greece to get to other European countries. The EU has sent border patrol teams to help guard the crossings. Many Greek companies hire illegal migrants to do a job because they do not have to pay them as much money as Greek workers.

Thousands of people protested outside the Greek parliament building about the government's plans for change.

Education

Every child in Greece gets free public education and must spend at least nine years at school. From the age of six, children must spend six years at primary school, called a *dimotiko*. Most primary schools start at 8:00 a.m. and finish at 2:00 p.m. Some schools in big cities, such as Athens, run a double-shift program, where some children go to school in the morning and some go to school in the afternoon.

Children at primary school learn the modern Greek language, mathematics, environmental studies, history, physical education, and art. As they move up in school they also learn a foreign language, culture, music, physics, and social studies.

After the school day is over, children may learn a sport such as tennis, go to the beach, or even be part of a Greek mythology club, where they can take part in storytelling, dancing, and singing.

Secondary school is divided into two sections. The first section is called *gymnasio,* and children have to spend three years here. The next section is called *lykeio,* and children can choose whether to complete this section or not. If they do complete *lykeio*, students can go on to a university or college.

YOUNG PEOPLE

During the summer, the Greek government organizes a "Teenager Parliament." This is where debates are held by young people. The **MPs** can learn what matters to young people, and the young people learn more about politics.

Primary school starts in September, and the school year finishes in June. Children must go to school five days a week. These children are rehearsing a dance for a public event in their village.

Health care

In the 1980s, the Greek government set up a national health care system, but there are also private hospitals. Greece's health care system is facing difficulties due to the current economic crisis. During 2010, there were strikes by doctors, nurses, and the people who supply hospitals with equipment and medicines over the payment they receive.

Transportation and communication

The ease of traveling in Greece depends on where you are trying to get to. It is only in the last 60 years or so that all of Greece's villages have become accessible to motorized traffic.

Getting around

The bus network in Greece is good and goes to even the tiniest of villages, even if it is just one bus a day. The rail network is only on the mainland and is slow. There are express highways that link the cities of Athens, Thessaloniki, Volos, and Patra, but some of the smaller roads can be very rough. There are 81 airports in Greece, and ferries link the many islands to each other and to the mainland.

Air pollution

Athens has a problem with air pollution, which gets worse in the hot summers. The Greek government has tried to improve the air quality by:
- expanding the subway system so people do not have to use their cars
- improving the bus schedules and adding special bus lanes
- controlling the number of cars entering the city. There is a system where cars with registration plates ending in an odd number are allowed to drive into the city center on one day, and those with even numbers are allowed the next day.

Athens is working to reduce its air pollution. On some days there is a complete ban on all traffic in the center of the city.

Communication

Today, a very large proportion of people in Greece own a mobile phone. The mobile phone allows even the most remote villager to be in touch with friends and family. Mobile phones are popular with young and old alike.

Greece is a wonderful mix of old and new. Even people in remote, traditional villages can keep in touch by mobile phone.

How to say...

Do you speak English?	*Μιλάτε Αγγλικά;*	(mee-LA-te AG-lee-ka?)
Where is...?	*Πού είναι...;*	(Pou EE-ne...?)
train station	*σταθμός τρένων*	(STATH-mo TREY-no)

Culture: Myths, Tradition, and Revival

Greece has a distinct culture. The ancient Greeks are known for their myths about gods and goddesses. Modern Greeks enjoy history, literature and arts, sports, and food.

Gods and goddesses

The ancient Greeks worshipped gods and goddesses. Greek mythology is a collection of ancient Greek stories about these gods. The stories were told by poets such as Homer and Hesiod. The gods and goddesses were thought to live on Mount Olympus. **Zeus** was the king of the gods, and his wife was the goddess Hera.

These Greek Orthodox priests are taking part in an Easter Procession through the streets of their town.

Religion

The main religion in Greece today is Greek Orthodoxy, which is a form of Christianity. Around 98 percent of people are Greek Orthodox. Around 1.3 percent are Muslim, as a result of Greece being under Turkish rule during the **Ottoman Empire** and the increasing number of immigrants from Muslim countries such as Turkey and Albania.

Festivals and holidays

There is a national holiday on March 25 to celebrate the Greeks becoming **independent** from the Ottoman Empire. Other festivals are connected to religion. For example, Greek Orthodox Easter is the most important religious festival in Greece. There are candlelight processions on Good Friday, fireworks on Easter Saturday, and then feasting, music, and dance on Easter Sunday.

Daily life

In the evening on Easter Saturday, everyone dresses up in their best clothes and goes to church. Children carry white candles or candles decorated with ribbons called *lambades*, which are bought for them by their godparents. At midnight, all lights are turned off and the priest appears with a candle, from which everyone lights their candles, so the church is filled with light.

The Greek Orthodox Church uses a different calendar. Most of us use the Gregorian calendar or New Calendar, but for Easter and other movable feasts, many Orthodox Churches use the Julian or Old Calendar. The Orthodox Church calendar starts on September 1 and ends on August 31.

Everyday life

Families are very important to the Greek way of life. Traditionally, the women would run the house and look after the children, and the men would go to work. Many sons will stay with their family until they get married.

Greek cafes, called *kafeneia*, are an important part of life in Greece. Traditionally, in villages and towns, these are places where the men would go to drink coffee, play backgammon, and chat. The women of the family would be busy at home. These *kafeneia* are also important as communication centers, because mail is collected here and telephone calls are made.

Food

For Greeks, eating is very much a social occasion to be enjoyed with family and friends. Much of Greek food reflects the centuries of Turkish rule, for example, sweets such as *baklava* and *kataifi*.

Meze is a selection of small dishes that is a bit like the Spanish tapas. You could eat *meze* as part of a lunch or dinner. Sometimes Greek friends will go out for *meze* and everyone will share the dishes. The word *meze* came from Turkey and is found in the countries that were part of the Ottoman Empire.

Even the smallest village will have a place to drink coffee and meet with others.

Tzatziki

Ask an adult to help you make this cool, refreshing dish. *Tzatziki* (zat-ZEE-key) is a popular dish made from cucumber and yogurt. It is often served with warm pita bread or with grilled meat and vegetables.

Ingredients

- 12 ounces (350 grams) Greek yogurt
- 1 cucumber
- 2 tablespoons lemon juice
- 2 cloves of garlic, grated finely
- extra virgin olive oil
- paprika, for sprinkling

What to do

1. Peel and de-seed the cucumber.
2. Grate the cucumber.
3. Drain the excess liquid from the grated cucumber using a fine cloth or mesh strainer.
4. Peel and then finely grate the garlic—be careful of your fingers.
5. Squeeze a lemon into a juicer or a cup.
6. Mix the yogurt, cucumber, lemon juice, and garlic in a mixing bowl.
7. Add a splash of extra virgin olive oil and mix in.
8. Put the Tzatziki into your serving dish and sprinkle with paprika (optional).

Poets and writers

Greece is known for its poets and writers. The ancient Greek poets and writers are especially well respected. Homer is perhaps the most influential writer in ancient Greek literature. He wrote two very famous works called the *Iliad* and the *Odyssey*. The *Illiad* is about the Trojan War, and the main character is Achilles. Achilles was an ancient Greek hero. The *Odyssey* is about a warrior called Odysseus. After ten years of fighting the war at Troy he spends another ten years trying to get back to his family.

More recently, two Greek poets have won the **Nobel Prize** for literature. In 1963, Giorgos Seferis won the Nobel Prize for poetry, and Odysseus Elytis won it in 1979. The Greek writer who is probably best known outside of Greece is Nikos Kazantzakis. In 1946 he wrote a book called *Zorba the Greek*, which was successful around the world.

NIKOS KAZANTZAKIS

(1883-1957)

Nikos Kazantzakis was born in Iraklion, Crete, in 1883. He grew up in a time when Crete was rebelling against the Ottoman government. Nikos Kazantzakis wrote many novels, but his longest work is a poem called *The Odyssey: A Modern Sequel*, after Homer's work. This poem fills 24 books and has 33,333 verses!

Greek music

Greek music has developed over many centuries and has been influenced by Greek history. Music from different regions has been influenced by Turkish, Balkan, and Italian music. One of the main types of traditional music is the *rebetiko*. These songs are accompanied by plucked string instruments, most popularly the *bouzouki*.

The bouzouki is a popular instrument in modern Greek music.

The Olympic Games

Greece is the birthplace of the Olympic Games. The ancient Greek games began in 776 BCE at Olympia in Greece. Olympia was thought to be a spiritual place and had temples for the god Zeus and goddess Hera. The first games were a way of honoring the gods and also a way of training for warfare. The Olympic Games were held every four years in honor of Zeus. The games began with running races, and over time sports such as wrestling, jumping, discus and javelin throwing, boxing, and chariot racing were added. The Olympic Games were so popular that *ekecheiria*, or truces, would be agreed to among the different groups of people who lived in Greece, so that athletes and spectators could travel to the games in safety.

This ancient Greek pottery shows athletes taking part in the ancient Olympic games.

Modern Games

The Olympic Games were revived in 1896 by Frenchman Baron Pierre de Coubertin. He founded the International Olympic Committee (IOC) in 1894, and two years later the modern Olympic Games were held in Athens, Greece. The Games were held there again in 2004.

This is the opening ceremony of the Olympic Games in Athens in 2004. The Games have been held every four years, with the exception of 1916, 1940, and 1944, when they were canceled because of World War I and World War II.

Greek sports today

As in many European countries, soccer (what they call football) is a popular sport in Greece. In 2004, Greece won the UEFA European Football (soccer) Championship. Basketball is also popular in Greece, and Greece's national team is considered to be one of the best in the world. Greece has also achieved success in volleyball, water polo, kickboxing, and weightlifting.

NIKOS GEORGALIS (BORN 1957)

Nikos is thought to be one of Europe's all-time greatest basketball players. In 2008, he was named one of the 50 Greatest Euroleague Contributors. Many people in Greece think that he has inspired thousands to take up basketball.

ELENI DANIILIDOU (BORN 1982)

Eleni Daniilidou was born on the island of Crete. She is a tennis player and has won five Women's Tennis Association (WTA) singles titles and one doubles title. She now lives in Thessaloniki, Greece.

Greece Today

Greece has an eventful history with four centuries of foreign rule. During the 20th century, there were wars and political instability with frequent government changes. These events caused many Greeks to leave Greece to go to live in another country. This has meant that Greek culture has spread around the world.

Territorial claims

Greece is now well established as a country in its own right, but there are still disputes with Turkey over boundaries, and especially over who owns the island of Cyprus. In 2011, talks among Greece, Turkey, and Cyprus were hopeful, and it looks as though progress is being made.

The Greek economy

Today, Greece is going through a difficult time economically. This will shape the way Greek people live. The Greek economy had to be rescued with some enormous international loans. There has been unrest about some of the reforms the government has brought in to try to save money. The **IMF** and **EU** have said that the savings the Greeks have made during this deep **recession** have been impressive, although the Greek government must make an extra effort to improve the situation. They have suggested that there should be better tax collection, cuts in the national health care system, and cuts in state-owned companies, such as the railways, which do not make a profit.

Despite all the challenges that history has thrown at them, the Greek people have achieved a lot. The history, landscape, and culture of this unique country will continue to attract visitors from around the world.

Greece is very much a part of the modern world. Here, an electric tram lets people travel quickly around the busy city of Athens.

Fact File

Official long name: Hellenic Republic (Hellas is the Greek name for Greece)

Official short name: Greece

Official language: Greek

Population: 10,749,943 (2010 estimate)

Currency: euro (€)

Capital city: Athens

Largest cities: Athens, Thessaloniki, Piraeus, Patras, Volos, Larissa, and Iraklion

Bordering countries: Albania, the Former Yugoslav Republic of Macedonia, Bulgaria, Turkey

Total area: 51,000 square miles (132,000 square kilometers)

Major rivers: Aliakmon, Axios, Strymon, Evros. None of Greece's rivers are navigable.

Highest point: Mount Olympus (9,570 feet, or 2,917 meters)

Lowest point: Mediterranean Sea (0 feet/meters)

Poverty rate: 20 percent of the Greek population live below the poverty line

Main exports: food and drink, manufactured goods, petroleum products, chemicals, textiles

Main imports: machinery, transportation equipment, fuels, chemicals

Main trading partners: Germany, Italy, Cyprus, Bulgaria, the United States, Turkey, China, France, Netherlands, South Korea, Belgium, Spain

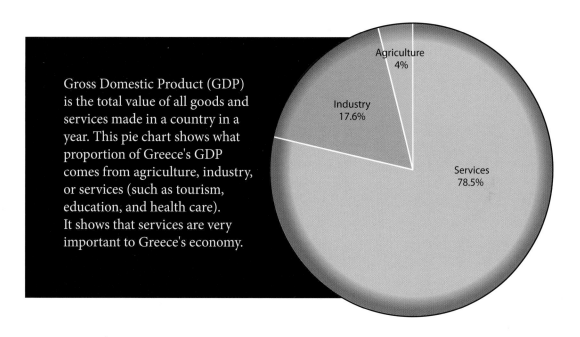

Gross Domestic Product (GDP) is the total value of all goods and services made in a country in a year. This pie chart shows what proportion of Greece's GDP comes from agriculture, industry, or services (such as tourism, education, and health care). It shows that services are very important to Greece's economy.

Agriculture 4%

Industry 17.6%

Services 78.5%

National anthem

By Dionysios Solomos (1823). Music by Nikos Mantzaros.
English translation by Rudyard Kipling.

We know thee of old
Oh divinely restored,
By the light of thine eyes
And the light of thy sword.

From the graves of our slain
Shall the valor prevail
As we greet thee,
As we greet thee again,
Hail, Liberty! Oh, Hail!

Famous Greeks: Prince Philip, Duke of Edinburgh (born 1921). Prince Philip is the husband of Queen Elizabeth II of England. He was born on the Greek island of Corfu. His family were exiled from Greece following the Greco-Turkish War. He married the Queen in 1947.

Maria Callas (1923–1977), opera singer. Callas was born in New York to Greek immigrant parents and moved back to Greece as a teenager. She became famous all over the world for her singing.

Karolos Papoulias (born 1929), current president of Greece.

Chryssa Mavromichali (born 1933), artist. Chryssa is famous for her sculptures using brilliantly colored neon tubing. Her works can be seen in buildings and collections many places around the world.

Christina Onassis (1950–1988), a famous heiress, born in New York to Aristotle Socrates Onassis and his wife Athina. Aristotle Onassis owned a Greek shipping empire, and the family is thought to be one of the wealthiest in the world.

George Papandreou (born 1952), current prime minister of Greece.

Sir Stelios Hadjioannou (born 1967), businessman, born in Athens to Greek-Cypriot parents. He is the founder of the EasyJet airline. This is a low-cost airline that revolutionized air travel in Europe.

Michalis Zambidis (born 1980), world champion professional kickboxer and martial artist. Zambidis is known to his fans as Iron Mike.

In ancient Greece, Mount Olympus was believed to be the home of the gods.

Timeline

BCE means "before the common era." When this appears after a date it refers to the number of years before the Christian religion began. BCE dates are always counted backward.

CE means "common era." When this appears after a date, it refers to the time after the Christian religion began.

7000–3000 BCE	Stone Age civilization in the area of the Aegean Sea
3000–1000 BCE	Bronze Age civilization in the area of the Aegean Sea
776 BCE	The first Olympic Games began in Olympia
500–400 BCE	Greek culture is the most advanced in the ancient world
336 BCE	Alexander the Great takes over as ruler of Greece
323 BCE	Alexander the Great dies and his **empire** is divided up
393 CE	Roman Emperor Theodosius I abolishes the Olympic Games
1950s	Greece is taken over by the Ottoman Empire
1829	Greece gains independence from the **Ottoman Empire**
1896	Frenchman Baron Pierre de Coubertin revives the modern Olympic Games
1922	King George II becomes king
1923	King George II goes into **exile** for the first time
1935	King George II returns from exile
1936	General Ioannis Metaxas's dictatorship begins
1940	Greece is invaded by Italy during World War II
1941	General Ioannis Metaxas dies
1941	George II is exiled from Greece for a second time

1941–1944	Greece is **occupied** by Germany
1946	King George II returns from exile to rule again
1946–1949	Greek **Civil War**
1946	*Zorba the Greek* is written by Nikos Kazantzakis
1947	King George II dies
1960	Great Britain, Greece, and Turkey agree that Cyprus is to be an **independent republic**
1963	Giorgos Seferis wins the **Nobel Prize** for poetry
1974	Attempted **coup** against President Makarios of Cyprus partly organized by Greek president, Dimitrios Ioannidis
	Ioannidis's regime collapses and Greece holds **democratic elections** to become a **parliamentary republic**
1981	Greece joins the **European Union (EU)**
1999	First National Marine Park is established to help protect the Loggerhead turtles
2010	The **International Monetary Fund** and **Eurozone governments** give Greece $147 billion in emergency loans

Glossary

antiroyalist person or group that is against having a king or queen as the head of their country

bauxite rock that is used to make aluminum

bulk carriers ships that carry large cargoes

Byzantine Empire eastern part of the Roman Empire

civil war war between people of the same country

communist member of the Communist party, which believes in state ownership of goods for the benefit of all

conquer overcome by force

coup violent and illegal seizure of power

democracy government of a country elected by its own people

democratic involving a system where people select the government

dictator leader who has complete power in a country and has not been elected by the people

disband break up; stop operating as a group

Economic Monetary Union (EMU) group of countries that all have the same currency, the euro

economic reform government policies brought in to try to improve a county's economy

election when the public votes on who will represent them in a government

empire group of countries governed by a single ruler

endangered species group of animals at risk from extinction

European Union (EU) international organization of European countries with shared political and economic aims. The EU formed from the EEC (European Economic Community) in 1993.

Eurozone governments seventeen member countries of the European Union who have the euro as their currency

exile banish someone from their own country as a punishment

gorge deep ravine with a river running through it

independent not controlled or supported. An independent country is not controlled by another country.

International Monetary Fund (IMF) organization of 187 countries that promotes international trade and financial stability

jackal wild animal, similar to a dog, found in Africa, Asia, and southeastern Europe

lobbying activities designed to influence other people

logging cutting and preparing forest timber

lynx medium-sized wildcat, found in parts of Asia, Europe, and North America

merchant fleet country's commercial shipping (for transporting goods to trade)

migrant person or animal who moves from one region or country to another

migration move from one region or country to another

monarchy type of government in which the head of the country is a king or queen

MP stands for member of parliament. MPs are elected by the people in their local area to represent them in parliament (like Congress). An MP can speak about issues in parliament, and can help to decide new laws.

Nobel Prize prize awarded for outstanding contributions to chemistry, physics, medicine, literature, economics, or peace. It is awarded annually and was established in 1901 by Alfred Nobel.

occupied country or territory under the control of a hostile army

Ottoman Empire founded in the 14th century by a Turkish tribal chieftain called Othman or Osman. The Empire lasted almost six centuries.

parliamentary republic type of republic that is governed by a parliament and prime minister

philosopher person who studies the meaning behind life and the universe. In ancient Greek times, a philosopher was someone who studied all aspects of the world around them.

recession period of economic decline

republic country ruled by an elected government and usually a president, and which does not have a king or queen

revolution the overturning pf a government by the people of a country, usually through the use of force and violence

species category in the classification system of living things; group of a particular type

WWF charity that used to be known as the World Wildlife Fund for Nature. The WWF helps to protect endangered animals and habitats.

Zeus king of the gods in Greek mythology

Find Out More

Books

Bartell, Jim. *Greece*. Minneapolis, MN: Bellwether Media, 2011.

Bingham, Jane. *Welcome to the Ancient Olympics*. Chicago: Raintree, 2007.

Claybourne, Anna. *Ancient Greece* (Time Travel Guide). Chicago: Raintree, 2007.

Etingoff, Kim. *Greece*. Broomall, PA: Mason Crest Publishers, 2005.

Green, Jen. *Greece*. Washington, DC: National Geographic Children's Books, 2009.

Zamosky, Lisa. *Greece: World Cultures Through Time*. Huntington Beach, CA: Teacher Created Materials, 2008.

DVD

Athens: Dawn of Democracy. Dir. Timothy Copestake. Perf. Bettany Hughes. PBS Home Video, 2007. DVD.

Websites

kids.nationalgeographic.com/kids/places/find/greece
Visit this website for facts and photos about Greece. The website also includes a short video about the Parthenon, showing how it used to look.

wwf.panda.org/what_we_do/endangered_species/marine_turtles/ loggerhead_turtle
Go to this website to find out more about the loggerhead turtles in Greece.

www.ancientgreece.co.uk
Visit this site to see famous artifacts from ancient Greece in the collection of the British Museum, including some sculptures originally from the Parthenon.

www.wwf.gr/en
Find out more about wildlife in Greece at this WWF website. Click on options in the "Working with nature" menu to find out more about endangered species, see beautiful photos of habitats in Greece, watch a video of a hatching turtle, or follow the path of a black vulture.

Places to visit in Greece

National Archaeological Museum of Athens
www.namuseum.gr/wellcome-en.html
This museum has an important collection of artifacts from around Greece.

Olympia
www.olympia-greece.org/site.html
Visit the Ancient Olympia Archaeological Site to see where the ancient Olympic Games began.

The Parthenon
www.theacropolismuseum.gr/?la=2
Visit the Parthenon in Athens to see what is left of the temple to Athena. The nearby Acropolis Museum contains many of the sculptures that were once part of the Parthenon.

The War Museum, Athens
www.warmuseum.gr/english
See displays from prehistoric times up to the present day. Find out more about the Greek War of Independence and World War II.

Places to visit in the United States

The Metropolitan Museum of Art, New York
www.metmuseum.org
Visit the Metropolitan Museum of Art in New York City to see a variety of ancient Greek artifacts.

The Getty Villa, California
www.getty.edu/visit/
The Getty Villa in Pacific Palisades, California, is dedicated to the study of ancient cultures, including Greece. Visit the website above to learn more about the Getty Villa and its collection.

Topic Tools

You can use these topic tools for your school projects. Trace the map onto a sheet of paper, using the black outline to guide you.

The Greek flag has five blue and four white stripes. A blue square with a white cross is in the upper left corner. The cross symbolizes Greek Orthodoxy, which is the religion of Greece. Copy the flag design and then color in your picture. Make sure you use the right colors!

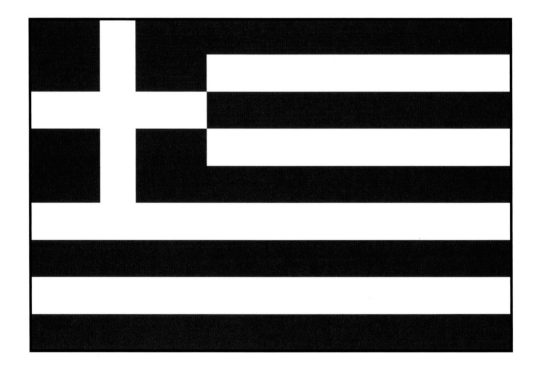

N

Athens

Index

Titles in the series